WALCH PUBLISHING

Daily Warm-Ups

SAT PREP
READING AND WRITING

Liza Kleinman

Level II

The classroom teacher may reproduce materials in this book for classroom use only.
The reproduction of any part for an entire school or school system is strictly prohibited.
No part of this publication may be transmitted, stored, or recorded in any form
without written permission from the publisher.

1   2   3   4   5   6   7   8   9   10
ISBN 0-8251-5877-X
Copyright © 2006
J. Weston Walch, Publisher
P.O. Box 658 • Portland, Maine 04104-0658
walch.com
Printed in the United States of America

Table of Contents

Introduction   *iv*

Essay Prompts 1

Vocabulary-in-Context 31

Sentence Completion 41

Passage-Based Reading 71

Identifying Sentence Errors 101

Improving Sentences 131

Improving Paragraphs 161

Answer Key 181

The *Daily Warm-Ups* series is a wonderful way to turn extra classroom minutes into valuable learning time. The 180 quick activities—one for each day of the school year—give students practice in answering questions in the reading and writing sections of the SAT. These daily activities may be used at the very beginning of class to get students into learning mode, near the end of class to make good educational use of that transitional time, in the middle of class to shift gears between lessons—or whenever else you have minutes that now go unused.

Daily Warm-Ups are easy-to-use reproducibles—simply photocopy the day's activity and distribute it. Or make a transparency of the activity and project it on the board. You may want to use the activities for extra-credit points or as a check on the test-taking skills that are built and acquired over time.

However you choose to use them, *Daily Warm-Ups* are a convenient and useful supplement to your regular lesson plans. Make every minute of your class time count!

Essay Prompts

Think carefully about the issue presented below and the assignment that follows.

Some people hold the belief that "power corrupts." They point out that history gives us many examples of leaders who have used their power irresponsibly. But many leaders have used their positions to accomplish good. Perhaps power is not a corrupting influence, but a magnifying glass that exaggerates the true nature of a leader.

ASSIGNMENT: Does power corrupt? Plan and write an essay in which you develop your point of view on this issue. Support your position with reasoning and examples taken from your reading, studies, experience, or observations.

1

Essay Prompts

> Think carefully about the issue presented below and the assignment that follows.

The philosopher George Santayana said, "Those who cannot remember the past are condemned to repeat it." This statement is certainly true; both individuals and governments who do not acknowledge the mistakes of the past find themselves unable to break free of harmful patterns.

ASSIGNMENT: Do you think that studying the past is the best way to plan for the future? Plan and write an essay in which you develop your point of view on this issue. Support your position with reasoning and examples taken from your reading, studies, experience, or observations.

2

Essay Prompts

Think carefully about the issue presented below and the assignment that follows.

The only way to learn is through experience. Knowledge gained through books is secondhand wisdom that is biased and flawed. Only through firsthand experience can people gain true knowledge and increase their understanding of the world in a meaningful way.

ASSIGNMENT: Is learning through experience usually the best way to learn? Plan and write an essay in which you develop your point of view on this issue. Support your position with reasoning and examples taken from your reading, studies, experience, or observations.

3

Essay Prompts

Think carefully about the issue presented below and the assignment that follows.

All acts of kindness are, at heart, acts of selfishness. People do not ever act solely for the benefit of others. They perform good deeds for the satisfaction they get from the experience. Acting for one's own satisfaction is, by definition, selfishness.

ASSIGNMENT: Do people perform good deeds out of selfishness? Plan and write an essay in which you develop your point of view on this issue. Support your position with reasoning and examples taken from your reading, studies, experience, or observations.

4

Essay Prompts

Think carefully about the issue presented below and the assignment that follows.

The old saying, "Money can't buy happiness" is quite true. People spend a great deal of money on items they don't need, convinced that these items will change their lives for the better. People who try to buy their way to happiness are destined to be disappointed.

ASSIGNMENT: Can money buy happiness? Plan and write an essay in which you develop your point of view on this issue. Support your position with reasoning and examples taken from your reading, studies, experience, or observations.

5

Essay Prompts

> Think carefully about the issue presented below and the assignment that follows.

A deeper appreciation of the arts creates stronger connections among people. Where there is a lack of art, poetry, and music, there is a lack of compassion, a lack of humanity. The arts remind us that we all share fundamental values and have common needs.

ASSIGNMENT: Do we need to study the arts in order to understand one another? Plan and write an essay in which you develop your point of view on this issue. Support your position with reasoning and examples taken from your reading, studies, experience, or observations.

6

Essay Prompts

Think carefully about the issue presented below and the assignment that follows.

The further technology advances, the less connected people are to one another. All of the gadgets intended to keep the lines of communication constantly open end up serving the opposite purpose: They create barriers that keep people at arm's length from one another.

ASSIGNMENT: Is technology changing for the worse the way people interact with one another? Plan and write an essay in which you develop your point of view on this issue. Support your position with reasoning and examples taken from your reading, studies, experience, or observations.

7

Essay Prompts

Think carefully about the issue presented below and the assignment that follows.

"He who hesitates is lost." This traditional saying is quite true. People need to seize opportunities when they arise. People who take too long mulling over their decisions end up having fewer opportunities than people who act immediately.

ASSIGNMENT: Do you think that it is better to act quickly and decisively than to spend a lot of time making a decision? Plan and write an essay in which you develop your point of view on this issue. Support your position with reasoning and examples taken from your reading, studies, experience, or observations.

8

Essay Prompts

Think carefully about the issue presented below and the assignment that follows.

Happiness is a matter of perception, not a set of circumstances. Too often, people believe that if they could only change a particular aspect of their lives, they would be happy. In fact, happy people often live in the same or worse conditions than unhappy people. Their happiness comes from their ability to look on the bright side.

ASSIGNMENT: Is happiness entirely a state of mind? Plan and write an essay in which you develop your point of view on this issue. Support your position with reasoning and examples taken from your reading, studies, experience, or observations.

9

Essay Prompts

Think carefully about the issue presented below and the assignment that follows.

We like to think that history is an exact record of what occurred in the past. However, there are always different sides to a story. No two people interpret events in exactly the same way, and any description of an event will be colored by the teller's point of view.

ASSIGNMENT: Can there be one, undisputed version of history? Plan and write an essay in which you develop your point of view on this issue. Support your position with reasoning and examples taken from your reading, studies, experience, or observations.

10

Essay Prompts

Think carefully about the issue presented below and the assignment that follows.

The old saying "the truth hurts" may be an appropriate warning. In some circumstances, it is better to conceal or doctor the truth. Whether the circumstances are personal or political, there is frequently a good argument to be made for hiding the truth.

ASSIGNMENT: Is it always best to be truthful? Plan and write an essay in which you develop your point of view on this issue. Support your position with reasoning and examples taken from your reading, studies, experience, or observations.

11

Essay Prompts

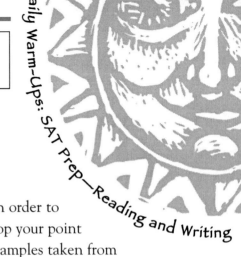

Think carefully about the issue presented below and the assignment that follows.

The best way to understand yourself is to spend time with people whose beliefs differ drastically from your own. It is only when you are forced to question your assumptions and defend your values that you can truly know your own mind.

ASSIGNMENT: Do we need to question our most basic beliefs in order to understand ourselves? Plan and write an essay in which you develop your point of view on this issue. Support your position with reasoning and examples taken from your reading, studies, experience, or observations.

12

Essay Prompts

Think carefully about the issue presented below and the assignment that follows.

Hardship brings out the best in people. Those who never know hardship never know what they are capable of achieving. In difficult times, people band together; in prosperous times, they believe themselves to be happy but live without the fundamental human connections forged through mutual dependence.

ASSIGNMENT: Does living through hardship make people happier? Plan and write an essay in which you develop your point of view on this issue. Support your position with reasoning and examples taken from your reading, studies, experience, or observations.

13

Essay Prompts

> Think carefully about the issue presented below and the assignment that follows.

There will always be those who resist change, believing that the old is better than the new. However, change is necessary and inevitable. Because of this, all change is a form of progress.

ASSIGNMENT: Is change always for the better? Plan and write an essay in which you develop your point of view on this issue. Support your position with reasoning and examples taken from your reading, studies, experience, or observations.

14

Essay Prompts

Think carefully about the issue presented below and the assignment that follows.

The expression "the grass is always greener on the other side of the fence" contains a great deal of truth. People are rarely satisfied with what they have. That's not necessarily bad, though. The desire to have or achieve more can motivate people to work harder and lead richer lives.

ASSIGNMENT: Is it human nature to want more than you have? Plan and write an essay in which you develop your point of view on this issue. Support your position with reasoning and examples taken from your reading, studies, experience, or observations.

15

Essay Prompts

Think carefully about the quotation presented below and the assignment that follows.

"Before you can inspire with emotion, you must be swamped with it yourself. Before you can move their tears, your own must flow. To convince them, you must yourself believe."

—Winston Churchill

ASSIGNMENT: What makes someone a good leader? Plan and write an essay in which you develop your point of view on this issue. Support your position with reasoning and examples taken from your reading, studies, experience, or observations.

16

Essay Prompts

Think carefully about the quotation presented below and the assignment that follows.

"Moral cowardice that keeps us from speaking our minds is as dangerous to this country as irresponsible talk. The right way is not always the popular and easy way. Standing for right when it is unpopular is a true test of moral character."

—Margaret Chase Smith

ASSIGNMENT: Can voicing unpopular ideas make a difference in the world? Plan and write an essay in which you develop your point of view on this issue. Support your position with reasoning and examples taken from your reading, studies, experience, or observations.

17

Essay Prompts

Think carefully about the issue presented below and the assignment that follows.

Failure should not be considered the end of the road; it is merely a signal that we need to find a new road. Throughout history, people have achieved success only after repeated failures. Often, those failures were crucial to the process.

ASSIGNMENT: Can failure lead to success? Plan and write an essay in which you develop your point of view on this issue. Support your position with reasoning and examples taken from your reading, studies, experience, or observations.

18

Essay Prompts

Think carefully about the issue presented below and the assignment that follows.

When our knowledge is limited to our own culture, it is difficult to really understand ourselves. How can we think critically about our culture's beliefs and behaviors if we have no other culture with which to compare ours?

ASSIGNMENT: Is it necessary to learn about other cultures in order for people to understand their own? Plan and write an essay in which you develop your point of view on this issue. Support your position with reasoning and examples taken from your reading, studies, experience, or observations.

19

Essay Prompts

> Think carefully about the issue presented below and the assignment that follows.

For U.S. citizens, voting is not just a right; it is a duty. When people fail to participate in their government, they relinquish their right to criticize their government or its decisions. In order for government to flourish, people must keep themselves informed and participate actively.

ASSIGNMENT: Do eligible voters have an obligation to vote? Plan and write an essay in which you develop your point of view on this issue. Support your position with reasoning and examples taken from your reading, studies, experience, or observations.

20

Essay Prompts

Think carefully about the issue presented below and the assignment that follows.

When something very important needs to be accomplished, it does not matter *how* it happens—it matters *whether* it happens. If a positive end result is achieved, whatever methods were used must be considered good and necessary.

ASSIGNMENT: Does the end result always justify the means by which it was obtained? Plan and write an essay in which you develop your point of view on this issue. Support your position with reasoning and examples taken from your reading, studies, experience, or observations.

21

Essay Prompts

> Think carefully about the issue presented below and the assignment that follows.

People sharing a common geographic area do not automatically create a community. When neighbors do not recognize each other on the street, when apartment-dwellers have no idea who lives above or below them, when everyone is anonymous to everyone else, we cannot call a place a community.

ASSIGNMENT: What makes a community? Plan and write an essay in which you develop your point of view on this issue. Support your position with reasoning and examples taken from your reading, studies, experience, or observations.

22

Essay Prompts

Think carefully about the issue presented below and the assignment that follows.

Perhaps money can't buy happiness, but it can certainly buy the things that make most people happy: adequate food, shelter, and health care; entertainment; vacations; and the possessions that so many of us want, even if we don't wish to admit it.

ASSIGNMENT: Can money buy happiness? Plan and write an essay in which you develop your point of view on this issue. Support your position with reasoning and examples taken from your reading, studies, experience, or observations.

23

Essay Prompts

Think carefully about the issue presented below and the assignment that follows.

"Don't look a gift horse in the mouth." This old expression means that if you're given a gift, you shouldn't question it—you should just accept it gratefully. But what if a gift is unwanted, or is even offensive to you? Are you obliged to be polite and accept it, or can you decline it?

ASSIGNMENT: Is it ever acceptable to decline a gift? Plan and write an essay in which you develop your point of view on this issue. Support your position with reasoning and examples taken from your reading, studies, experience, or observations.

24

Essay Prompts

Think carefully about the issue presented below and the assignment that follows.

Former First Lady Eleanor Roosevelt said, "No one can make you feel inferior without your consent." This statement is true; if you are self-confident and secure, no one can make you feel otherwise.

ASSIGNMENT: Do you think that it is possible for someone to make you feel insecure if you don't already feel insecure? Plan and write an essay in which you develop your point of view on this issue. Support your position with reasoning and examples taken from your reading, studies, experience, or observations.

25

© 2006 Walch Publishing

Essay Prompts

> Think carefully about the issue presented below and the
> assignment that follows.

The presence of television in the courtroom is consistent with the
ideal of the public's right to know.

ASSIGNMENT: Should television be allowed in the courtroom? Is it
part of the public's right to know, or does television create a theatrical
atmosphere in the courtroom? Plan and write an essay in which you develop
your point of view on this issue. Support your position with reasoning and examples
taken from your reading, studies, experience, or observations.

26

Essay Prompts

Think carefully about the issue presented below and the assignment that follows.

The old saying, "Happiness is a journey, not a destination" is quite true. Happiness is now, but many convince themselves that life will be better "after something." People should realize that there is no better time to be happy than right now.

ASSIGNMENT: Do you think that happiness is the experience of living life every day? Plan and write an essay in which you develop your point of view on this issue. Support your position with reasoning and examples taken from your reading, studies, experience, or observations.

27

Essay Prompts

> Think carefully about the issue presented below and the assignment that follows.

We all know what heroes and heroines are. According to the dictionary, they are people who are admired for their great deeds, bravery, or noble qualities. But hero worship now comes in many forms.

ASSIGNMENT: What is your definition of a hero? Plan and write an essay in which you develop your point of view on this issue. Support your position with reasoning and examples taken from your reading, studies, experience, or observations.

28

Essay Prompts

> Think carefully about the quotation presented below and the assignment that follows.

"Imagination is more important than knowledge."

—Albert Einstein

ASSIGNMENT: Is an active imagination more important than knowledge? Plan and write an essay in which you develop your point of view on this issue. Support your position with reasoning and examples taken from your reading, studies, experience, or observations.

29

Essay Prompts

> Think carefully about the quotation presented below and the assignment that follows.

"I've learned that people will forget what you said, people will forget what you did, but people will never forget how you made them feel."

—Maya Angelou

ASSIGNMENT: Can the way you treat people have more of an effect on people than what you say to them? Plan and write an essay in which you develop your point of view on this issue. Support your position with reasoning and examples taken from your reading, studies, experience, or observations.

30

Vocabulary-in-Context

Select the best answer to the following question.

At the end of a long, exhausting day, the physicist was anxious to go home to bed.

In the line above, "anxious" most nearly means

(A) uneasy

(B) afraid

(C) eager

(D) concerned

(E) worried

31

Vocabulary-in-Context

Select the best answer to the following question.

Some scholars believe that William Shakespeare's genius had less to do with encyclopedic knowledge than with common sense and intuition.

In the lines above, "encyclopedic" most nearly means

        (A) literary

        (B) specialized

        (C) fundamental

        (D) comprehensive

        (E) abridged

32

Vocabulary-in-Context

Select the best answer to the following question.

When questioned by the media, the young man stated that the very concept of competing in a triathlon was an idea foreign to him.

In the line above, "concept" most nearly means

(A) plan

(B) notion

(C) image

(D) completion

(E) beginning

Vocabulary-in-Context

Select the best answer to the following question.

Embodied in the social idiosyncrasies of a rural Mississippi county, William Faulkner's astute observations still have currency in the modern-day south.

In the lines above, "currency" most nearly means

      (A) funds

      (B) style

      (C) unusualness

      (D) relevance

      (E) importance

Vocabulary-in-Context

Select the best answer to the following question.

The young duke had no fortune. He had been fortunate to receive an inheritance, but spending freely what had come freely, had realized nothing.

In the lines above, "realized" most nearly means

(A) accomplished

(B) fulfilled

(C) learned

(D) understood

(E) accumulated

35

Vocabulary-in-Context

Select the best answer to the following question.

The professor has an intense knowledge of the playwright's works, and he will not entertain any doubt concerning their authorship.

In the lines above, "entertain" most nearly means

        (A) engage

        (B) occupy

        (C) consider

        (D) amuse

        (E) seize

36

Vocabulary-in-Context

Select the best answer to the following question.

Some people who invested in the booming dot com market of the 1990s were disappointed; few of the businesses appreciated in value.

In the lines above, "appreciated" most nearly means

(A) minimized

(B) declined

(C) spiraled

(D) compounded

(E) increased

37

Vocabulary-in-Context

Select the best answer to the following question.

Winston Churchill's determination of spirit can be seen in the way he nobly led England in a time of war, although he was pressed by others to support appeasement policies.

In the lines above, "pressed" most nearly means

    (A) urged

    (B) compelled

    (C) required

    (D) suggested

    (E) enforced

38

Vocabulary-in-Context

Select the best answer to the following question.

After the horror of 9/11, some would say that we will never be safe again—that achieving 100% safety is probably impossible in a free society. But I trust that no one in this vast assemblage of security personnel will agree with those sentiments.

In the lines above, "sentiments" most nearly means

(A) emotions

(B) beliefs

(C) threats

(D) objections

(E) loyalties

39

© 2006 Walch Publishing

Vocabulary-in-Context

Select the best answer to the following question.

In the movie, the jewel thieves made their escape by scaling the mansion's walls and stealing away under the cover of darkness.

In the lines above, "stealing" most nearly means

(A) robbing

(B) grabbing

(C) slipping

(D) abducting

(E) taking

© 2006 Walch Publishing

Sentence Completion

Select the word that best completes the sentence.

Toward the end of the twentieth century, many fiction writers experimented with minimalism, a style that favored ---- prose over dense, wordy writing.

(A) intelligent

(B) spare

(C) meaningful

(D) interesting

(E) fresh

41

© 2006 Walch Publishing

Sentence Completion

Select the words that best complete the sentence.

Before refrigerators were widely ----, the harvesting and exporting of ice from rivers and ponds to other states was a ---- part of the New England economy.

(A) available...sizeable

(B) discovered...needed

(C) used...mild

(D) known...minute

(E) built...certain

42

Sentence Completion

Select the words that best complete the sentence.

The bill's supporters argued that it would ---- the amount of money brought into the state, while causing a ---- amount of inconvenience to local residents.

(A) reduce...small

(B) effect...sizeable

(C) supplement...measured

(D) increase...minimal

(E) bolster...significant

43

Sentence Completion

Select the word that best completes the sentence.

Despite the ---- mass of dark clouds gathering overhead, the teams decided to start their game, hoping to finish before the rain fell.

(A) alluring

(B) retreating

(C) dissipating

(D) harmless

(E) foreboding

44

Sentence Completion

Select the word that best completes the sentence.

Unlike her sister, who often exaggerated the truth, Linda was ---- in recounting the exact details of a situation.

(A) delicate

(B) determined

(C) scrupulous

(D) careless

(E) indifferent

45

Sentence Completion

Select the words that best complete the sentence.

The melody's apparent ---- was ---- ; the piece was actually quite complicated and extremely difficult to master.

(A) intricacy...common

(B) complexity...unfounded

(C) simplicity...deceptive

(D) ease...obvious

(E) lucidity...enduring

46

Sentence Completion

Select the word that best completes the sentence.

Leonardo da Vinci, though best known for his paintings, was also a ---- inventor, whose designs included architecture, weapons, and various types of conveyances including flying machines.

(A) reluctant

(B) prolific

(C) limited

(D) destructive

(E) collaborative

47

Sentence Completion

Select the words that best complete the sentence.

Although it might be tempting to confuse anecdotes with evidence, tales of a remedy's ---- are not necessarily ---- that the product works.

(A) necessity...determinations

(B) failures...assurances

(C) safety...standards

(D) effectiveness...proof

(E) powers...citations

48

Sentence Completion

Select the word that best completes the sentence.

The first telegraph wires to cross the Atlantic Ocean ---- communication; suddenly, messages could be relayed in a matter of minutes rather than weeks.

(A) transformed

(B) delayed

(C) entertained

(D) restrained

(E) invented

49

Sentence Completion

Select the words that best complete the sentence.

Though generally a ---- person, Marie found herself growing ----
listening to her friends' long, detailed stories about their vacation.

(A) jealous...envious

(B) kind...understanding

(C) curious...unhappy

(D) polite...indifferent

(E) patient...restless

50

Sentence Completion

Select the word that best completes the sentence.

The feuding countries found that through ---- , they could resolve more of their differences than they could through aggression.

(A) investigation

(B) deterioration

(C) diplomacy

(D) dispute

(E) patronage

Sentence Completion

Select the word that best completes the sentence.

While Austen's writing focuses on narrow domestic concerns, its close examination of Edwardian social customs ---- to the reader a broad sense of what it was like to live back then.

(A) provides

(B) insists

(C) remembers

(D) instructs

(E) refers

52

Sentence Completion

Select the words that best complete the sentence.

Morgan's calm, ---- manner ---- his true feelings, which were anything but tranquil.

(A) satisfied...reflected

(B) agitated...showed

(C) belligerent...enhanced

(D) passive...belied

(E) reflective...invoked

Sentence Completion

Select the words that best complete the sentence.

Although publicly the mayor spoke ---- of his town, in private,
he was less ---- , pointing out the many difficulties it had yet
to overcome.

(A) glowingly...enthusiastic

(B) insultingly...measured

(C) fondly...interested

(D) reverentially...unhappy

(E) excitedly...mysterious

Sentence Completion

Select the words that best complete the sentence.

The use of technology is an important ---- to our curriculum, but we should not allow it to ---- the main course material.

(A) addition...enhance

(B) supplement...overshadow

(C) effort...obscure

(D) adjustment...dictate

(E) detractor...undermine

Sentence Completion

Select the word that best completes the sentence.

Madeline had expected the reception to her speech to be ---- at best; she was stunned when the audience stood up to applaud her for several minutes.

(A) exaggerated

(B) hearty

(C) enthusiastic

(D) unwelcome

(E) tepid

56

Sentence Completion

Select the words that best complete the sentence.

Although Mike's car was several decades old and in less than ---- condition, it was still ---- to transport him to and from work each day.

(A) perfect...unable

(B) useable...necessary

(C) pristine...sufficient

(D) inhabitable...needed

(E) shameful...helping

© 2006 Walch Publishing

Sentence Completion

Select the word that best completes the sentence.

Javanese shadow puppet shows are not just a form of entertainment; they are believed to be one of the world's oldest continuous story-telling traditions, ---- centuries' worth of history, religion, and culture.

(A) preserving

(B) shielding

(C) inventing

(D) belittling

(E) implying

58

Sentence Completion

Select the word that best completes the sentence.

Hikers should check to see whether the trails they intend to travel are open to the public, because recent wet weather has ---- some of them.

(A) reinforced

(B) beautified

(C) deleted

(D) reclaimed

(E) eroded

59

© 2006 Walch Publishing

Sentence Completion

Select the words that best complete the sentence.

The nature of the ---- was twofold; people argued about whether the town council had the right to approve a new building, and if it did, whether the construction plans should ---- .

(A) agreement...unfurl

(B) inference...count

(C) situation...falter

(D) conflict...proceed

(E) assignment...halt

60

Sentence Completion

Select the words that best complete the sentence.

Due to the island's ---- the mainland, it had retained its own distinct culture and customs.

(A) affinity for

(B) dependence upon

(C) isolation from

(D) proximity to

(E) similarity to

61

Sentence Completion

Select the words that best complete the sentence.

Determined to ---- the expectations of his parents, who believed that he was less capable than his brother, Paul studied hard and, as a result, ---- in all his classes.

(A) avoid...floundered

(B) entertain...succeeded

(C) believe...failed

(D) exceed...excelled

(E) reclaim...stagnated

62

Sentence Completion

Select the word that best completes the sentence.

Gish Jen's novel *Typical American* ---- a Chinese immigrant's struggle to achieve the American dream by opening a modest restaurant and moving his family to the suburbs.

(A) belies

(B) entails

(C) contrasts

(D) informs

(E) chronicles

© 2006 Walch Publishing

Sentence Completion

Select the word that best completes the sentence.

While many people believe that the platypus is ---- in its status as an egg-laying mammal, the spiny anteater, a mammal, lays eggs as well.

(A) unique

(B) unwavering

(C) ambiguous

(D) uncertain

(E) impaired

Sentence Completion

Select the words that best complete the sentence.

The country's history had been ---- , but the new leadership, dedicated to rebuilding a strong economy, promised a ---- future.

(A) uncertain...wavering

(B) turbulent...stable

(C) uneventful...similar

(D) intense...workable

(E) trying...frivolous

65

Sentence Completion

Select the words that best complete the sentence.

Good food does not have to be ---- prepared; some of the most elegant meals are also the ---- .

(A) neatly...blandest

(B) elaborately...simplest

(C) carefully...most painstaking

(D) quickly...easiest

(E) stylishly...tastiest

66

Sentence Completion

Select the words that best complete the sentence.

Unlike her documentaries, the director's new film dispenses with ---- and introduces the viewer to a whimsical and ---- world.

(A) artistry...creative

(B) silliness...somber

(C) regulations...ordered

(D) realism...improbable

(E) cynicism...harrowing

Sentence Completion

Select the word that best completes the sentence.

Novels of the Victorian era often depict the struggle of women to find romantic love, despite the fact that marriage was, at that time, largely a ---- institution that ensured a woman's financial stability and social respectability.

(A) magical

(B) searing

(C) nonexistent

(D) failing

(E) practical

Sentence Completion

Select the words that best complete the sentence.

The company president's subordinates regarded her highly because, in spite of her powerful position, she was both ---- and ---- .

(A) preoccupied...accepting

(B) unaware...anxious

(C) approachable...empathetic

(D) overpowering...understanding

(E) servile...authoritative

Sentence Completion

Select the word that best completes the sentence.

This time of year, storms tend to be ---- ; it's hard to predict exactly what course one will take, or how much damage it might do.

(A) erratic

(B) foreseeable

(C) vague

(D) impressionable

(E) inflexible

70

Passage-Based Reading

> Read the passage, and then select the best answer to the question.

In southern Florida lies a vast area of wetlands, the Florida Everglades. Before present-day efforts to preserve the area's fragile ecosystems, people saw an opportunity for development. At the end of the nineteenth century, people believed they could transform this land from wetland to dry fields by draining the water through canals. Those fields would be excellent for farming.

The passage suggests that

(A) because the wetlands were not successfully drained, there would be no need for modern-day preservation efforts

(B) in the late nineteenth century, the interests of farmers were at odds with the interests of conservationists

(C) people of the last century were very concerned about conservation

(D) the idea of transforming the Everglades from wetland to farmland would not be considered a good one in the present day

(E) none of the ecosystems that originally existed in the Florida Everglades exists today

71

© 2006 Walch Publishing

Passage-Based Reading

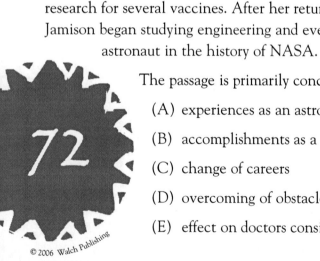

Read the passage, and then select the best answer to the question.

Before she ventured into space, Mae C. Jamison made a tremendous impact right here on Earth. After her graduation from medical school, she served in the Peace Corps in Sierra Leone and Liberia, West Africa, as a medical officer. There, she supervised medical staff, provided care, and implemented health and safety guidelines. She also worked with the Centers for Disease Control on research for several vaccines. After her return from the Peace Corps, Jamison began studying engineering and eventually became the first black female astronaut in the history of NASA.

The passage is primarily concerned with Jamison's

(A) experiences as an astronaut

(B) accomplishments as a medical officer

(C) change of careers

(D) overcoming of obstacles

(E) effect on doctors considering joining the Peace Corps

72

Passage-Based Reading

Read the passage, and then select the best answer to the question.

He knew that no matter how well he prepared, no matter how many times he rehearsed the speech in his mind, something would happen to make him lose his equilibrium. The last time he'd lectured, it had been an audience member who had fallen asleep, right in front of him. The time before that, the microphone had not worked. He had spent the entire presentation bellowing futilely into a cavernous auditorium. Something was bound to go wrong this time, too. There was no point in even trying to guess what that would be. All he could do was wait and see, and wish that the speech were over already.

The lecturer's feelings can best be summed up as

(A) dread

(B) terror

(C) confusion

(D) hope

(E) despair

Passage-Based Reading

Read the passage, and then select the best answer to the question.

In the following paper, I will be discussing the relationship between traditional American white music and traditional American black music. Specifically, I will examine the roots from which the two traditions derive, emphasizing their similarities and differences. I will then demonstrate how the two traditions, while remaining distinct from each other, nonetheless greatly influenced each other.

The primary purpose of the paragraph is to

74

(A) argue a point

(B) compare two points of view

(C) explain a decision

(D) justify an opinion

(E) introduce a topic

Passage-Based Reading

Read the passage, and then select the best answer to the question.

The invention of the daguerreotype in 1839 paved the way for modern photography. The invention ushered in a new era. Painted portraits of the powerful and famous had always been popular. By the middle of the nineteenth century, thanks to the relative ease of use and affordability of the daguerreotype, members of the middle class, too, could have their portraits made.

The passage suggests that

(A) by the mid-1800s, people no longer wanted to view painted portraits

(B) few members of the middle class had their portraits made before the mid-1800s

(C) if the daguerreotype had been invented earlier, there would have been a larger middle class

(D) unlike modern photographs, daguerreotypes could only be used to take portraits

(E) poor people were uninterested in looking at portraits of the wealthy

75

Passage-Based Reading

Read the passage, and then select the best answer to the question.

It may look as though a honeybee's flight is random, but in fact, it is a form of language. Honeybees use different movements, which scientists refer to as "dances," to provide information to one another about the location and quality of food sources. The dances are very distinct from one another and carry specific messages. For example, the "waggle dance" communicates the location of a food source more than 35 yards away; the "round dance" communicates the location when the source is less than 35 yards away.

The author mentions the "waggle dance" and the "round dance" in order to

(A) contrast two completely different behaviors

(B) challenge a commonly-held belief

(C) illustrate a point about honeybees

(D) make a generalization about insects

(E) refute the notion that honeybees can communicate

Passage-Based Reading

Read the passage, and then select the best answer to the question.

While Earth Day has existed only since 1970, the idea of a nationally recognized day that addresses environmental concerns is not new. In the late 1800s, Arbor Day and Bird Day were established. Over the following decades, they were observed primarily by schoolchildren, who learned about the value of protecting and preserving natural resources. Earth Day is part of a long tradition of holidays that celebrate the natural environment.

The author mentions a "long tradition" in order to

(A) compare Earth Day to the holidays that preceded it

(B) suggest that Earth Day is a poor replacement for Arbor Day and Bird Day

(C) emphasize that Earth Day is not new or unique in its focus

(D) encourage the reader to celebrate Earth Day

(E) explain why people no longer recognize Arbor Day or Bird Day

77

Passage-Based Reading

> Read the passage, and then select the best answer to the question.

The genre of pulp fiction enjoyed wide popularity from the 1920s to the 1950s. The name "pulp fiction" comes from the pulpy, low-quality paper on which it was printed. Each magazine specialized in one type of writing, such as romance, horror, or detective stories. They had a reputation for being affordable, lurid, and entertaining. Often, well-known writers who needed extra income wrote for pulp fiction magazines under assumed names.

The last sentence suggests that

(A) famous authors thought that writing for pulp fiction magazines would harm their reputations

(B) pulp fiction magazines were the only chance writers had for publication

(C) pulp fiction magazines paid their authors extremely well

(D) only highly accomplished authors had a chance at getting their work published in pulp fiction magazines

(E) authors who wrote for pulp fiction magazines assumed that their readers knew who they were

Passage-Based Reading

> Read the passage, and then select the best answer to the question.

Children might be benefiting from some high-tech toys and gadgets, computers, and video games. Perhaps they are gaining useful skills, such as eye-hand coordination. But I disagree that time spent with these toys, supplemented with time spent in highly structured activities such as sports leagues, constitutes child-appropriate playtime. What happened to the days of exploration, of children creating games and amusements? What happened to children following their own inclinations and entertaining themselves? Children who are dragged from activity to activity, or mindlessly immersed in electronic games, are missing out not only on some of the joys of childhood, but also on the opportunity to learn how to be self-reliant in the absence of pre-manufactured fun.

The author mentions sports leagues as an example of

(A) a way for children to get more exercise

(B) a child-appropriate activity

(C) a healthy but dull activity

(D) an activity that detracts from children's creativity

(E) the worst way that children can spend their time

79

Passage-Based Reading

Read the passage, and then select the best answer to the question.

While the Wright brothers are generally given credit for being the fathers of modern air travel, they owe a great debt to Otto Lilienthal, who wrote extensively about flight during the later part of the nineteenth century. He was the first to create a working glider—a carefully engineered set of wings that carried him from a high leap across a distance of about eighty feet. He also constructed several flying machines of increasing sophistication. His ideas directly influenced the Wright brothers, who first built gliders and, eventually, a machine that ran on gasoline engine power.

The passage suggests that the difference between Lilienthal's flying machines and the Wright brothers' was that

(A) the Wright brothers put a great deal of thought into their flying machine, whereas Lilienthal stumbled upon his by luck

(B) the Wright brothers' flying machine was successful, but Lilienthal's was not

(C) Lilienthal was concerned only with conquering distance, not altitude

(D) the Wright brothers built one flying machine, while Lilienthal made several

(E) the Wright brothers' machine used fuel and Lilienthal's did not

Passage-Based Reading

Read the passage, and then select the best answer to the question.

The National American Women Suffrage Association, an organization that campaigned for the right of American women to vote, was formed in 1890. The Association was formed when two different organizations, formerly rivals, merged. One of the organizations, the National Woman Suffrage Association, believed in gaining suffrage through a federal constitutional amendment. The other organization, the American Woman Suffrage Association, believed that the best way to achieve the goal of women's suffrage was to wage individual state campaigns. The newly formed organization combined these tactics and secured the right to vote for American women in 1920.

The passage suggests that before merging, the two organizations disagreed about

(A) whether women should have the right to vote

(B) the proper time frame for achieving the goal of suffrage

(C) the best person to lead the new organization

(D) the reason that suffrage was important

(E) the best strategy for achieving the goal of suffrage

81

Passage-Based Reading

> Read the passage, and then select the best answer to the question.

You are walking on a beach at night. You kick at the wet sand as you go, and suddenly the air is filled with bright green sparks. You wade a little way into the ocean, and with each movement of the water, there is a small fireworks show.

What you are witnessing is called bioluminescence, a phenomenon in which a chemical reaction within living organisms creates light. Certain single-cell organisms in the sea will produce this reaction when agitated. The result can be both startling and beautiful to look at.

The opening paragraph serves primarily to

- (A) give a scientific explanation for a phenomenon
- (B) advocate a particular course of action
- (C) dramatize a phenomenon in order to highlight it
- (D) demonstrate the need for increased science education
- (E) compare different types of sea life

Passage-Based Reading

Read the passage, and then select the best answer to the question.

The question, Jake knew, was not whether his family would ask about his future plans, but when they would. It happened at every family gathering: Someone—an aunt, his grandfather, one of his cousins—would ask him what he was planning to do after graduation. Jake didn't know why they bothered asking; the answer he gave was always the same. He didn't know. What he did not say was that he did, in fact, have one firm plan: He was not, absolutely not, going to join the family business. He knew they suspected this—why else would they keep asking? It was like a contest to see which side would crack first and bring up the subject directly. Jake was growing weary of the charade.

The "charade" referred to in the last sentence most nearly means

(A) chase

(B) game

(C) uncertainty

(D) tension

(E) attempt

83

Passage-Based Reading

Read the passage, and then select the best answer to the question.

The world's first written language was created over 5,000 years ago by the Sumerians, who lived in what is now southern Iraq. This language, called cuneiform, originated from the use of pictures to represent objects. Originally, the pictures were rather detailed, closely resembling the objects they represented. Over time, the pictures grew simpler, eventually becoming the abstract marks of cuneiform writing. These marks could indicate sounds or even sophisticated concepts.

The passage suggests that a characteristic of written language is that

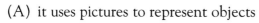

(A) it uses pictures to represent objects

(B) it can be easily understood

(C) it can convey ideas, not just objects

(D) it evolves over time

(E) it represents and preserves cultural values

84

Passage-Based Reading

Read the passage, and then select the best answer to the question.

Theodore Seuss Geisel is well known as Dr. Seuss, the author of many beloved children's books, including *The Cat in the Hat.* Less well known is his work as a political cartoonist. From 1941–1943, Geisel was the chief editorial cartoonist for *PM*, a New York newspaper. During that time, Geisel created over 400 political cartoons that commented on the social issues of the day, which largely revolved around World War II and the United States' involvement in it.

According to the passage, Theodore Seuss Geisel

(A) was widely misunderstood in his day

(B) had little talent as a cartoonist, so he became a children's book author

(C) was an active spokesman against war

(D) had a career that has been largely overlooked

(E) thought of himself as a political activist more than a children's book author

85

© 2006 Walch Publishing

Passage-Based Reading

> Read the passage, and then select the best answer to the question.

In conclusion, both domestic cats and domestic dogs retain strong similarities to their wild ancestors. From the dog's pack allegiance to the cat's hunting instinct, we can see in our pets the traits that increased an animal's likelihood for survival in the wild. The more we learn about the behavior of wild canines and felines, the better we can negotiate our shared living space with their descendants.

Which of the following would most likely be found earlier in this essay?

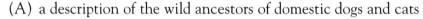

(A) a description of the wild ancestors of domestic dogs and cats

(B) a list of all the animals that people like to keep as pets

(C) a discussion of which wild birds can be domesticated

(D) an argument that domestic animals should be returned to the wild

(E) a detailed history of famous cats and dogs

86

Passage-Based Reading

Read the passage, and then select the best answer to the question.

In the 1920s and 30s, New York City's Harlem was home to a surge in African American cultural expression. This surge, termed the "Harlem Renaissance," was in part the result of a large wave of migration of Southern African Americans to Northern cities. The Harlem Renaissance was an artistic, political, literary, and musical movement giving voice to a people historically disenfranchised from mainstream American culture.

The author of this passage would most likely agree with which of the following?

(A) The Harlem Renaissance would have occurred even without the large number of immigrants from the south.

(B) Before the 1920s, much of American popular culture had ignored or excluded the experiences of African Americans.

(C) The Harlem Renaissance was the first historical period in which African Americans sought to have the same rights and privileges as white Americans.

(D) Before the 1920s, mainstream American literature, art, and music accurately reflected the mix of cultures in America.

(E) The Harlem Renaissance caused the Civil Rights movement.

87

Passage-Based Reading

Read the passage, and then select the best answer to the question.

Those late afternoons in summer, the moist, hot air grew particularly heavy. The sky went nearly dark with steel-gray clouds. A thin breeze threaded through the trees, causing the leaves to stir in warning, and then the first fat drops began to fall. At first, we could see the individual dark marks the drops left, and then they speeded up, until the asphalt turned color completely and we became, as our parents later said, "soaked through to the bone." The grown people vanished indoors immediately, but we remained outside until the last possible second, which was when we saw that first jagged streak of lightning in the distance; then our courage failed, or our parents called, and we scattered into our respective houses.

88

The narrator's description of the parents serves to

(A) contrast the children's and adults' reactions to the storm

(B) explain the relationship between the narrator and her parents

(C) discourage children from playing outside during thunder storms

(D) argue that there is an unbridgeable gap between adults and children

(E) imply that the narrator's parents disapproved of her choices

© 2006 Walch Publishing

Passage-Based Reading

Read the passage, and then select the best answer to the question.

Think how much more high school students could learn if, rather than spending all day with people of their own age and experience level, they were in a more integrated society. After all, life outside of school consists of a broad mix of people; are students really gaining from their time spent in an artificial hierarchy of essentially similar people? Should they not interact with people who have different values, different experiences, different points of view?

In this passage, the author makes the assumption that

(A) young children do not need to experience the diversity that older students do

(B) high school students do not want to interact with anyone other than their peers

(C) high school serves as a stepping stone to college entrance

(D) all high school students are similar to one another

(E) teachers do not wish to expose students to a broad range of viewpoints

89

© 2006 Walch Publishing

Passage-Based Reading

Read the passage, and then select the best answer to the question.

Polar bears, contrary to what many people think, do not have white fur. The fur is, in fact, transparent and free of pigment, with a hollow core. This hollow core reflects visible light in the same manner that snow does, making the polar bears appear to be white. In 1979, three polar bears at California's San Diego Zoo turned a startling shade of green. The cause turned out to be algae growing in the hollow cores of the bears' hair. The bears were treated with a saline solution, which killed the algae and returned the bears to their normal appearance.

The author uses the example of the algae in the bears' fur to emphasize

(A) the wide array of unexpected problems that zookeepers face

(B) the possibility that polar bears sometimes have pigmented fur

(C) the likelihood that animals placed in zoos will suffer

(D) the need for further research into the origin of polar bears' white color

(E) the fact that polar bears' color does not come from pigment in their fur

90

Passage-Based Reading

Read the passage, and then select the best answer to the question.

What is a fresco? Some of the most famous paintings in the world are frescoes. Yet, these special paintings are not found in picture frames. In fact, a fresco is a very special type of painted wall or ceiling. Frescoes are sometimes confused with murals. Murals, however, are not necessarily frescoes. A mural can be painted directly onto the surface of a wall with oil, acrylic, or even watercolor paint. A mural can also first be painted onto canvas and then attached to a wall with glue. In both cases, the mural is a painting that lies on the outer surface of the wall. A true fresco, on the other hand, is actually painted *into* the wall material itself.

The primary purpose of the paragraph is to

(A) argue a point

(B) compare two types of paintings

(C) explain the process of painting

(D) justify an opinion about frescoes

(E) introduce a topic

91

Passage-Based Reading

Read the passage, and then select the best answer to the question.

In order to paint a true fresco, the painter first prepares fresh plaster. A coat of the wet plaster is then applied to a section of wall or ceiling. The artist paints directly onto the plaster before it dries, using pure pigment. As the plaster dries, it absorbs the color and then hardens, providing an excellent casing for the artist's work.

The word "pigment" in the fourth line of the paragraph means

(A) paint

(B) plaster

(C) color

(D) dye

(E) none of the above

92

Passage-Based Reading

Read the passage, and then select the best answer to the question.

Although she later became known for her writings about the sea, Rachel Carson was born in 1907 far from the coast, in the hill country of western Pennsylvania. She grew up in a simple farmhouse, learning about the world of nature—particularly local bird life—under her mother's enthusiastic guidance. The youngest of three children, Rachel was a quiet, shy child who spent much of her time reading and writing. At the age of ten, she was thrilled to see one of her poems published in *Saint Nicholas,* a popular children's magazine of the time. Throughout her school and college years, Rachel continued to write and to submit her work to publishers.

The genre that best describes this paragraph is

(A) autobiography

(B) fable

(C) biography

(D) short story

(E) parable

93

© 2006 Walch Publishing

Passage-Based Reading

> Read the passage, and then select the best answer to the question.

In 1901, an expedition led by Robert Falcon Scott set out to explore the South Pole on the ship *Discovery*. The following is adapted from *The Voyages of Captain Scott* by Charles Turley.

Christmas Day found the ship in the open expanse of the Southern Ocean. Normally, the *Discovery* had little to fear from the worst winds. But at this time she was so heavily loaded that if she had encountered heavy seas, the results would have been very unpleasant. Much of her cargo would have been lost, and the ship's structure would have been in great danger.

Fine weather continued, though, and on January 3 Scott and his companions crossed the Antarctic Circle. They did not realize how long a time would pass before they would return.

Why was the *Discovery* in more danger than usual from heavy winds?

(A) The ship was traveling in uncharted territory.

(B) The ship was traveling at a very high speed.

(C) The water in that area was unusually cold, and the seas were rough.

(D) The ship carried a very heavy load.

(E) The ship's structure was inherently weak.

94

Passage-Based Reading

Read the passage, and then select the best answer to the question.

Progress [of the *Discovery*] became slow, but life abounds on the ice. The birds that came to visit the ship were a source of much interest. The pleasantest and most constant of these visitors was the small snow petrel, with its dainty snow-white feathers, black beak and feet, and black, beady eyes. These little birds abound in the pack ice. The squeak of the penguin was constantly heard, often long before the birds were seen. Curiosity drew them to the ship. As the ship forced her way onward, these little visitors would again and again leap into the water, eager to discover what this strange sight could be. —adapted from *The Voyages of Captain Scott*, Charles Turley

The passage is important because it

(A) explains the importance for the explorers to reach the Antarctic

(B) contrasts the sailors' life back home and their life aboard the *Discovery*

(C) provides details that help the reader understand what it was like to spend time on the *Discovery*

(D) describes the research that the explorers performed in the Antarctic Circle

(E) illustrates the life of sailors of the twentieth century

95

Passage-Based Reading

Read the passage, and then select the best answer to the question.

In all parts of the ice pack seals are plentiful and spend long hours asleep on the ice. The commonest kind is the crab-eater or white seal, but the Ross seal is not rare, and here and there is found the sea-leopard, ranging wide and preying on the penguins. It is curious to observe that both seals and penguins believe themselves to be safe when out of the water. In the sea they are running risks all the time, and in that element Nature has made them swift to hunt or to avoid being preyed upon. But once on ice or land they have known no enemy, and cannot therefore imagine one. —adapted from *The Voyages of Captain Scott*, Charles Turley

The tone of the paragraph can best be described as

(A) extreme distaste

(B) angry accusation

(C) strong admiration

(D) mild disinterest

(E) amused interest

96

Passage-Based Reading

> Read the passage, and then select the best answer to the question.

In this passage adapted from *Great Expectations* by Charles Dickens, the hero—Pip—recalls a dismal period of his youth.

It is a most miserable thing to feel ashamed of home . . . . Home had never been a very pleasant place to me, because of my sister's temper. But Joe had sanctified it and I believed in it. I had believed in the best parlor as a most elegant salon; I had believed in the front door as a mysterious portal of the Temple of State whose solemn opening was attended with a sacrifice of roast fowls; I had believed in the forge as the glowing road to manhood. Now, it was all coarse and common, and I would not have had Miss Havisham and Estella see it on any account.

The passage can best be described as

(A) a criticism of a young person's attitude

(B) an analysis of lowly living conditions

(C) a description of a young boy's relationship with others

(D) an account of the reflections of a young boy's emotional state

(E) a defense of working class life

97

Passage-Based Reading

Read the passage, and then select the best answer to the question.

It is a most miserable thing to feel ashamed of home. . . . Home had never been a very pleasant place to me, because of my sister's temper. But Joe had sanctified it and I believed in it. I had believed in the best parlor as a most elegant salon; I had believed in the front door as a mysterious portal of the Temple of State whose solemn opening was attended with a sacrifice of roast fowls; I had believed in the kitchen as a chaste though not magnificent apartment; I had believed in the forge as the glowing road to manhood. Now, it was all coarse and common, and I would not have had Miss Havisham and Estella see it on any account.
—adapted from *Great Expectations*, Charles Dickens

The narrator's discontent with his home at this time was caused by

(A) a false sense of pride he had about his home

(B) Miss Havisham and Estella's impression of the home

(C) an awareness of how his home would appear to others

(D) his sister's temper

(E) the lack of refinement of the kitchen of the house

98

Passage-Based Reading

Read the passage, and then select the best answer to the question.

Once, it had seemed to me that when I should at last roll up my shirt-sleeves and go into the forge, Joe's 'prentice, I should be distinguished and happy. Now the reality was in my hold, I only felt that I was dusty with the dust of small coal, and that I had a weight upon my daily remembrance to which the anvil was a feather. There have been occasions in my later life (I suppose as in most lives) when I have felt for a time as if a thick curtain had fallen on all its interest and romance, to shut me out from anything save dull endurance any more.
—adapted from *Great Expectations*, Charles Dickens

It can be inferred that the narrator has been apprenticed to

(A) a blacksmith

(B) a cook

(C) a grave digger

(D) a booksmith

(E) a hairdresser

Passage-Based Reading

Read the passage, and then select the best answer to the question.

Once, it had seemed to me that when I should at last roll up my shirt-sleeves and go into the forge, Joe's 'prentice, I should be distinguished and happy. Now the reality was in my hold, I only felt that I was dusty with the dust of small coal, and that I had a weight upon my daily remembrance to which the anvil was a feather. There have been occasions in my later life (I suppose as in most lives) when I have felt for a time as if a thick curtain had fallen on all its interest and romance, to shut me out from anything save dull endurance any more.

—adapted from *Great Expectations*, Charles Dickens

In the passage, the narrator's mood can most specifically be described as

(A) excited

(B) happy

(C) unhappy

(D) cautious

(E) spirited

100

Identifying Sentence Errors

The following sentence may contain an error in grammar, usage, choice of words, or idioms. If an underlined word or phrase is incorrect, choose that letter. If the sentence is correct, choose E, <u>No error</u>.

Folk tales <u>from different</u> cultures often use similar
              A

<u>plots and characters</u>, which <u>they</u> have been painstakingly
       B   C

<u>catalogued by folklorists</u>. <u>No error</u>
      D   E

101

Identifying Sentence Errors

The following sentence may contain an error in grammar, usage, choice of words, or idioms. If an underlined word or phrase is incorrect, choose that letter. If the sentence is correct, choose E, <u>No error</u>.

<u>No matter</u> how much they disagreed or <u>what their</u> personal
  A   B

<u>preference is</u>, the artists <u>managed</u> to work together to come up
    C   D

with one vision for the mural. <u>No error</u>
                                 E

102

Identifying Sentence Errors

The following sentence may contain an error in grammar, usage, choice of words, or idioms. If an underlined word or phrase is incorrect, choose that letter. If the sentence is correct, choose E, <u>No error</u>.

Delia and Carlos <u>decided</u> to become <u>a doctor</u> after they
                         A   B

<u>participated in</u> a community health program <u>that provided</u> care
        C   D

to the elderly. <u>No error</u>
                        E

103

Identifying Sentence Errors

The following sentence may contain an error in grammar, usage, choice of words, or idioms. If an underlined word or phrase is incorrect, choose that letter. If the sentence is correct, choose E, <u>No error</u>.

Long before either computers <u>and</u> typewriters <u>existed</u>, scribes
               A   B

<u>carefully wrote</u> out manuscripts by hand, <u>which meant that</u>
  C   D

relatively few were produced. <u>No error</u>
                       E

104

Identifying Sentence Errors

The following sentence may contain an error in grammar, usage, choice of words, or idioms. If an underlined word or phrase is incorrect, choose that letter. If the sentence is correct, choose E, <u>No error</u>.

Every evening, the curator of the exhibit <u>has</u> to check that
                                           A

everyone has left the gallery, <u>then</u> pick up any trash that viewers
                                B

<u>have dropped</u>, then <u>sets the alarm</u> before leaving for the night.
      C   D

<u>No error</u>
   E

105

Identifying Sentence Errors

The following sentence may contain an error in grammar, usage, choice of words, or idioms. If an underlined word or phrase is incorrect, choose that letter. If the sentence is correct, choose E, <u>No error</u>.

In <u>order</u> to master a new instrument, one <u>must practice</u> every day,
   A   B

<u>and</u>, if possible, <u>you</u> should listen to recordings of other musicians.
C   D

<u>No error</u>
   E

106

Identifying Sentence Errors

The following sentence may contain an error in grammar, usage, choice of words, or idioms. If an underlined word or phrase is incorrect, choose that letter. If the sentence is correct, choose E, No error.

The cellist Yo Yo Ma <u>has mastered</u> a wide variety of <u>musical styles</u>,
                        A   B

including classical, bluegrass, and <u>plays</u> traditional Brazilian
                                            C

<u>melodies</u>. <u>No error</u>
  D   E

107

Identifying Sentence Errors

The following sentence may contain an error in grammar, usage, choice of words, or idioms. If an underlined word or phrase is incorrect, choose that letter. If the sentence is correct, choose E, <u>No error</u>.

The <u>company's decision</u> about whether or not to raise prices
          A

will <u>most likely be</u> determined by a <u>combination</u> of its costs and
     B   C

the prices of <u>its competitors</u>. <u>No error</u>
         D   E

108

Identifying Sentence Errors

The following sentence may contain an error in grammar, usage, choice of words, or idioms. If an underlined word or phrase is incorrect, choose that letter. If the sentence is correct, choose E, <u>No error</u>.

Although Daniel had a great <u>interest in</u> the <u>history of</u> American
                            A   B

musical theater, it had never before <u>occurred</u> to him that he could
                                  C

<u>make a career</u> out of his hobby. <u>No error</u>
     D   E

109

Identifying Sentence Errors

The following sentence may contain an error in grammar, usage, choice of words, or idioms. If an underlined word or phrase is incorrect, choose that letter. If the sentence is correct, choose E, <u>No error</u>.

For years, the university's deans <u>had been</u> struggling to understand
                                                  A

why, <u>in spite of</u> a rising workplace <u>demand for</u> degrees, fewer of the
        B   C

state's <u>students were</u> attending college. <u>No error</u>
                    D   E

110

Identifying Sentence Errors

The following sentence may contain an error in grammar, usage, choice of words, or idioms. If an underlined word or phrase is incorrect, choose that letter. If the sentence is correct, choose E, <u>No error</u>.

The harmful effects of smoking <u>has been</u> known <u>for years</u>, but,
                                  A   B

in spite of the evidence <u>directly</u> linking smoking to disease,
                                   C

<u>people continue</u> to take up the habit. <u>No error</u>
     D   E

111

© 2006 Walch Publishing

Identifying Sentence Errors

The following sentence may contain an error in grammar, usage, choice of words, or idioms. If an underlined word or phrase is incorrect, choose that letter. If the sentence is correct, choose E, <u>No error</u>.

Despite <u>months of negotiations</u>, the union and the electric company
             A

<u>were</u> no closer to reaching <u>an agreement</u> that would meet the needs of
B   C

the workers and <u>also is</u> acceptable to the company's board of directors.
              D

    <u>No error</u>
      E

112

Identifying Sentence Errors

> The following sentence may contain an error in grammar, usage, choice of words, or idioms. If an underlined word or phrase is incorrect, choose that letter. If the sentence is correct, choose E, <u>No error</u>.

Because <u>there is</u> ample discussion of the new policies <u>before</u> they
$\qquad$ A $\qquad\qquad\qquad\qquad\qquad\qquad$ B

<u>were enacted</u>, the employees feel that they were treated <u>fairly</u> by
$\quad$ C $\qquad\qquad\qquad\qquad\qquad\qquad\qquad\qquad$ D

their supervisor. <u>No error</u>
$\qquad\qquad\qquad$ E

Identifying Sentence Errors

The following sentence may contain an error in grammar, usage, choice of words, or idioms. If an underlined word or phrase is incorrect, choose that letter. If the sentence is correct, choose E, <u>No error</u>.

The <u>fiction of</u> Jamaica Kincaid, <u>who grew up</u> on the island of
     A   B

Antigua, often <u>explores</u> the effect of English <u>culture on</u> colonized
                C   D

Caribbean islands. <u>No error</u>
                 E

114

Identifying Sentence Errors

The following sentence may contain an error in grammar, usage, choice of words, or idioms. If an underlined word or phrase is incorrect, choose that letter. If the sentence is correct, choose E, <u>No error</u>.

Coral reefs, <u>found</u> in tropical oceans worldwide, <u>is</u> in danger from a
      A   B

variety of <u>environmental</u> factors, <u>including</u> land development and
            C   D

over-harvesting. <u>No error</u>
          E

115

Identifying Sentence Errors

The following sentence may contain an error in grammar, usage, choice of words, or idioms. If an underlined word or phrase is incorrect, choose that letter. If the sentence is correct, choose E, <u>No error</u>.

The <u>researchers hoped</u> that the result of their experiment <u>would</u> be
　　　　A　　　　　　　　　　　　　　　　　　　　　　　B
either to disprove a long-standing theory <u>and</u> to provide evidence
　　　　　　　　　　　　　　　　　　　　　C
that further research <u>needed</u> to be done. <u>No error</u>
　　　　　　　　　　　D　　　　　　　　　　E

116

Identifying Sentence Errors

The following sentence may contain an error in grammar, usage, choice of words, or idioms. If an underlined word or phrase is incorrect, choose that letter. If the sentence is correct, choose E, <u>No error</u>.

<u>Because some</u> people believe <u>strongly</u> in lucky charms, trinkets
    A   B

that they <u>believe</u> bring good fortune, others dismiss them as
            C

<u>superstitious nonsense</u>. <u>No error</u>
      D   E

117

Identifying Sentence Errors

The following sentence may contain an error in grammar, usage, choice of words, or idioms. If an underlined word or phrase is incorrect, choose that letter. If the sentence is correct, choose E, <u>No error</u>.

<u>Among</u> the many topics <u>discussed at</u> the town meeting <u>was</u> the
 A   B   C
upcoming mayoral election <u>and</u> the proposed recycling plant.
                                             D

<u>No error</u>
 E

Identifying Sentence Errors

The following sentence may contain an error in grammar, usage, choice of words, or idioms. If an underlined word or phrase is incorrect, choose that letter. If the sentence is correct, choose E, No error.

The <u>rapid</u> changing <u>field of</u> evolutionary genetics <u>proved</u> to be
　　　A　　　　　　　　B　　　　　　　　　　　　　C
exactly the challenge that Maria <u>had hoped</u> it would be when she
　　　　　　　　　　　　　　　　　D
entered the profession. <u>No error</u>
　　　　　　　　　　　　　　E

119

Identifying Sentence Errors

> The following sentence may contain an error in grammar, usage, choice of words, or idioms. If an underlined word or phrase is incorrect, choose that letter. If the sentence is correct, choose E, <u>No error</u>.

Impressed by the proposal we had <u>written</u>, the foundation agreed
                                   A

to <u>provide funding</u> for <u>Emily and I</u> to teach <u>creative</u> dance to
     B   C   D

elementary school students. <u>No error</u>
                               E

120

Identifying Sentence Errors

The following sentence may contain an error in grammar, usage, choice of words, or idioms. If an underlined word or phrase is incorrect, choose that letter. If the sentence is correct, choose E, <u>No error</u>.

The committee <u>found</u> it more difficult to plan the community
             A

art project, <u>which</u> involved <u>coordinating artists</u> of all ages and
        B   C

abilities, than <u>carrying</u> it out. <u>No error</u>
           D   E

121

Identifying Sentence Errors

The following sentence may contain an error in grammar, usage, choice of words, or idioms. If an underlined word or phrase is incorrect, choose that letter. If the sentence is correct, choose E, <u>No error</u>.

Advertisements <u>try to</u> convince consumers that a particular
                  A
<u>product can</u> work miracles, <u>but</u> many people are not as gullible
      B   C
<u>than</u> advertisers would like. <u>No error</u>
  D   E

Identifying Sentence Errors

The following sentence may contain an error in grammar, usage, choice of words, or idioms. If an underlined word or phrase is incorrect, choose that letter. If the sentence is correct, choose E, <u>No error</u>.

Visitors to the museum <u>is</u> strongly <u>encouraged</u> to interact with the
                      A   B

exhibits, <u>which</u> were created to <u>provide a realistic</u> and memorable
        C   D

experience. <u>No error</u>
         E

123

Identifying Sentence Errors

The following sentence may contain an error in grammar, usage, choice of words, or idioms. If an underlined word or phrase is incorrect, choose that letter. If the sentence is correct, choose E, <u>No error</u>.

There <u>were several</u> key pieces of evidence <u>presented during</u> the
      A   B

trial; of all of them, the most convincing <u>was</u> the <u>tape from</u> a
                                       C   D

surveillance camera. <u>No error</u>
                   E

124

Identifying Sentence Errors

The following sentence may contain an error in grammar, usage, choice of words, or idioms. If an underlined word or phrase is incorrect, choose that letter. If the sentence is correct, choose E, <u>No error</u>.

Later, the journalist <u>would compile</u> his notes into a cohesive,
                            A

detailed <u>narrative</u> <u>about his travels</u>, but for now, he scribbled brief
          B   C

<u>observations</u> on scraps of paper. <u>No error</u>
   D   E

125

Identifying Sentence Errors

> The following sentence may contain an error in grammar, usage, choice of words, or idioms. If an underlined word or phrase is incorrect, choose that letter. If the sentence is correct, choose E, <u>No error</u>.

While gorillas have a reputation <u>for being</u> fierce, they are
A

actually gentle, peaceful creatures who may make frightening

<u>noises when threatened</u> but rarely <u>to confront</u> other <u>animals</u> . <u>No error</u>
B C D E

126

Identifying Sentence Errors

The following sentence may contain an error in grammar, usage, choice of words, or idioms. If an underlined word or phrase is incorrect, choose that letter. If the sentence is correct, choose E, <u>No error</u>.

<u>Because of</u> <u>newer and more accurate</u> information,
   A   B

<u>doctors' recommendations</u> for treating certain illnesses
          C

are different <u>from earlier decades</u>. <u>No error</u>
          D   E

127

Identifying Sentence Errors

The following sentence may contain an error in grammar, usage, choice of words, or idioms. If an underlined word or phrase is incorrect, choose that letter. If the sentence is correct, choose E, <u>No error</u>.

After the <u>students</u> <u>had went</u> to observe the recycling plant,
        A   B

<u>they put together</u> a presentation about <u>their</u> findings. <u>No error</u>
   C   D   E

128

Identifying Sentence Errors

The following sentence may contain an error in grammar, usage, choice of words, or idioms. If an underlined word or phrase is incorrect, choose that letter. If the sentence is correct, choose E, <u>No error</u>.

While it helps to have some <u>familiarity with</u> different musical
$\qquad\qquad\qquad\qquad\qquad\qquad$ A

styles, extensive knowledge <u>is not</u> a requirement <u>in taking</u> the
$\qquad\qquad\qquad\qquad\qquad$ B $\qquad\qquad\qquad\qquad$ C

music appreciation <u>class</u>. <u>No error</u>
$\qquad\qquad\qquad$ D $\qquad$ E

© 2006 Walch Publishing

Identifying Sentence Errors

The following sentence may contain an error in grammar, usage, choice of words, or idioms. If an underlined word or phrase is incorrect, choose that letter. If the sentence is correct, choose E, <u>No error</u>.

<u>Available in</u> the guidance counselor's office <u>are</u> a list of summer
    A   B

jobs and internships, <u>some of which</u> are paid positions and some
                         C

of which <u>provide valuable</u> experience but no salary. <u>No error</u>
           D   E

130

Improving Sentences

Choose the best way to revise the underlined part of the sentence. Your choice should make the most effective sentence and express the meaning of the original sentence. If no revision is needed, choose (A), which repeats the original underlined sentence part.

Anna Mary Robertson Moses sold her first painting <u>and she was seventy-seven years old at the time</u>.

(A) and she was seventy-seven years old at the time

(B) at age of seventy-seven years

(C) at the time she was seventy-seven

(D) upon the time she reached seventy-seven years

(E) when she was seventy-seven

Improving Sentences

Choose the best way to revise the underlined part of the sentence. Your choice should make the most effective sentence and express the meaning of the original sentence. If no revision is needed, choose (A), which repeats the original underlined sentence part.

By routing the new highway around the town instead of through the middle of it, the governor prevented an excess of traffic noise, <u>this was a concern of the townspeople</u>.

(A) this was a concern of the townspeople

(B) it was thought by the townspeople to be a concern

(C) because the townspeople had concerns

(D) a concern of the townspeople

(E) being the concern the townspeople were having

132

Improving Sentences

Choose the best way to revise the underlined part of the sentence. Your choice should make the most effective sentence and express the meaning of the original sentence. If no revision is needed, choose (A), which repeats the original underlined sentence part.

The city was famous not just for its beauty and charm, but <u>it has a</u> tradition of hospitality.

(A) it has a

(B) as well is its

(C) also for its

(D) having also a

(E) having too

133

Improving Sentences

Choose the best way to revise the underlined part of the sentence. Your choice should make the most effective sentence and express the meaning of the original sentence. If no revision is needed, choose (A), which repeats the original underlined sentence part.

Jake, Tanya, and Nina were exploring the forest when <u>she, looking up at the top of the trees, spotted an owl</u>.

(A) she, looking up at the top of the trees, spotted an owl

(B) Nina, looking up at the top of the trees, spotted an owl

(C) Nina looked up at the top of the trees, because she spotted an owl

(D) she looked up at the top of the trees and Nina spotted an owl

(E) Nina, since she looked up at the top of the trees, she spotted an owl

134

Improving Sentences

Choose the best way to revise the underlined part of the sentence. Your choice should make the most effective sentence and express the meaning of the original sentence. If no revision is needed, choose (A), which repeats the original underlined sentence part.

Scheduled to leave the station in five minutes, <u>Carrie ran breathlessly toward the train, which stood waiting by the platform</u>.

(A) Carrie ran breathlessly toward the train, which stood waiting by the platform

(B) Carrie's breathless run was toward the train, which stood waiting by the platform

(C) waiting by the platform was the train and Carrie ran breathlessly toward it

(D) a train stood waiting by the platform Carrie ran breathlessly toward it

(E) the train stood waiting by the platform, and Carrie ran breathlessly toward it.

135

Improving Sentences

Choose the best way to revise the underlined part of the sentence. Your choice should make the most effective sentence and express the meaning of the original sentence. If no revision is needed, choose (A), which repeats the original underlined sentence part.

The meeting had barely begun <u>and that was when it was announced by the president of the company</u> that she would be stepping down.

(A) and that was when it was announced by the president of the company

(B) and then the president of the company announced

(C) when the president of the company announced

(D) and then they all learned from the president of the company

(E) and then the announcement was made by the president of the company

136

Improving Sentences

Choose the best way to revise the underlined part of the sentence. Your choice should make the most effective sentence and express the meaning of the original sentence. If no revision is needed, choose (A), which repeats the original underlined sentence part.

Assessing the health of the bay will require testing <u>where they</u> will study the long-term changes in temperature and salinity.

(A) where they

(B) through which volunteers

(C) for which some

(D) which they

(E) and the volunteers

137

Improving Sentences

Choose the best way to revise the underlined part of the sentence. Your choice should make the most effective sentence and express the meaning of the original sentence. If no revision is needed, choose (A), which repeats the original underlined sentence part.

While some scientists claim that intelligent animals can learn to communicate in sign language, others maintain that language <u>is an inherently human trait that animals can only mimic</u>.

(A) is an inherently human trait that animals can only mimic

(B) being an inherently human trait, animals can only be able to mimic it

(C) in contrast to other beliefs is an inherently human trait and animals can only mimic it

(D) that is only mimicked by animals is an inherently human trait

(E) which is an inherent trait in humans can be mimicked only by animals

138

Improving Sentences

Choose the best way to revise the underlined part of the sentence. Your choice should make the most effective sentence and express the meaning of the original sentence. If no revision is needed, choose (A), which repeats the original underlined sentence part.

<u>With only a few more</u> to go, the cyclists pushed toward the end of the race.

(A) With only a few more

(B) Having only a few more

(C) With only a few more laps

(D) Aware of their being only a few more

(E) Because of the laps being a few more

139

© 2006 Walch Publishing

Improving Sentences

Choose the best way to revise the underlined part of the sentence. Your choice should make the most effective sentence and express the meaning of the original sentence. If no revision is needed, choose (A), which repeats the original underlined sentence part.

Aldous Huxley's novel *Brave New World* painted a chilling picture of <u>a future society in which</u> the government mass-produced people to fill particular, predetermined roles.

(A) a future society in which

(B) a future society, being when

(C) a society which, being in the future,

(D) a society of the future because in it

(E) a future for society since in it

140

Improving Sentences

Choose the best way to revise the underlined part of the sentence. Your choice should make the most effective sentence and express the meaning of the original sentence. If no revision is needed, choose (A), which repeats the original underlined sentence part.

<u>Along with being valued for its beautiful color and scent</u>, lavender plants might contain some medicinal properties.

(A) Along with being valued for its beautiful color and scent

(B) Still having been valued for their beautiful color and scent

(C) While also they are valued for its beautiful color and scent

(D) In addition to having a beautiful color and scent,

(E) As well as they have a beautiful color and scent

141

Improving Sentences

Choose the best way to revise the underlined part of the sentence. Your choice should make the most effective sentence and express the meaning of the original sentence. If no revision is needed, choose (A), which repeats the original underlined sentence part.

Tasha took a drawing class last year, <u>and she has been sketching portraits of her friends ever since.</u>

(A) and she has been sketching portraits of her friends ever since

(B) since the time that she has been sketching portraits of her friends

(C) where since then she has been sketching portraits of her friends

(D) she has been sketching portraits of her friends ever since

(E) and now since then she has been sketching portraits of her friends

142

Improving Sentences

Choose the best way to revise the underlined part of the sentence. Your choice should make the most effective sentence and express the meaning of the original sentence. If no revision is needed, choose (A), which repeats the original underlined sentence part.

A tornado, one of the most violent types of <u>storms, a rotating column of air that extends</u> between a thunderstorm and the ground.

(A) storms, a rotating column of air that extends

(B) storms, is a rotating column of air that extends

(C) storms, being a rotating column of air that is extending

(D) storms, that is a rotating column of air extending

(E) storms, it rotates a column of air to extend

143

Improving Sentences

Choose the best way to revise the underlined part of the sentence. Your choice should make the most effective sentence and express the meaning of the original sentence. If no revision is needed, choose (A), which repeats the original underlined sentence part.

The new conservation center, <u>providing a protected natural environment for an array of native species, and will</u> encourage student visits from local schools.

(A) providing a protected natural environment for an array of native species, and will

(B) provides a protected natural environment for an array of native species, will

(C) providing a protected natural environment for an array of native species, will

(D) to provide a protected natural environment, will for an array of native species

(E) in providing a protected natural environment for an array of native species, is to

144

Improving Sentences

Choose the best way to revise the underlined part of the sentence. Your choice should make the most effective sentence and express the meaning of the original sentence. If no revision is needed, choose (A), which repeats the original underlined sentence part.

No sooner had the show ended <u>but the network was flooded with calls</u> from viewers requesting more information about the topic.

(A) but the network was flooded with calls

(B) but the network had then been flooded with calls

(C) than the network had been flooded with calls

(D) than having been flooded with calls, the network

(E) than the network was flooded with calls

145

Improving Sentences

Choose the best way to revise the underlined part of the sentence. Your choice should make the most effective sentence and express the meaning of the original sentence. If no revision is needed, choose (A), which repeats the original underlined sentence part.

The facilitator should keep the discussion on track <u>but also with a goal to encourage</u> creative thinking and unusual solutions.

(A) but also with a goal to encourage

(B) while encouraging

(C) but while trying also to encourage

(D) aiming at the same time to encourage

(E) the goal should also be to encourage

146

Improving Sentences

Choose the best way to revise the underlined part of the sentence. Your choice should make the most effective sentence and express the meaning of the original sentence. If no revision is needed, choose (A), which repeats the original underlined sentence part.

In light of new fossil discoveries, which point to the existence of a previously unknown species, scientists <u>to revise</u> their understanding of migration patterns.

(A) to revise

(B) have been to revise

(C) revising

(D) are revising

(E) has revised

147

Improving Sentences

Choose the best way to revise the underlined part of the sentence. Your choice should make the most effective sentence and express the meaning of the original sentence. If no revision is needed, choose (A), which repeats the original underlined sentence part.

Lacking good directions, <u>my arrival at the job interview was later</u> than I had hoped.

   (A) my arrival at the job interview was later

   (B) I arrived hopefully later

   (C) it was later when I arrived at the job interview

   (D) the later it was when I arrived at the job interview

   (E) I arrived at the job interview later

148

Improving Sentences

Choose the best way to revise the underlined part of the sentence. Your choice should make the most effective sentence and express the meaning of the original sentence. If no revision is needed, choose (A), which repeats the original underlined sentence part.

The novelist Alice Walker, whose celebrated fiction depicts the lives of African American women, <u>is an active participant in</u> environmental and political causes.

(A) is an active participant in

(B) in which she actively participates

(C) actively participating in

(D) of which she actively participates

(E) being a participant in actual

149

Improving Sentences

Choose the best way to revise the underlined part of the
sentence. Your choice should make the most effective sentence
and express the meaning of the original sentence. If no revision
is needed, choose (A), which repeats the original underlined
sentence part.

By reading the enclosed instructions carefully, <u>mistakes can be
avoided</u> when setting up a new piece of equipment.

      (A) mistakes can be avoided

      (B) by avoiding mistakes

      (C) you can avoid mistakes

      (D) your mistakes will be avoided

      (E) they will help you avoid mistakes

150

Improving Sentences

Choose the best way to revise the underlined part of the sentence. Your choice should make the most effective sentence and express the meaning of the original sentence. If no revision is needed, choose (A), which repeats the original underlined sentence part.

No one is <u>more happier than me</u> to hear the news of your good fortune.

(A) more happier than me

(B) happier than I

(C) happy like myself

(D) happier but me

(E) as happy like I feel

151

© 2006 Walch Publishing

Improving Sentences

Choose the best way to revise the underlined part of the sentence. Your choice should make the most effective sentence and express the meaning of the original sentence. If no revision is needed, choose (A), which repeats the original underlined sentence part.

One of the committee's most controversial ideas <u>were that the organization's president should have</u> a fixed term limit.

(A) were that the organization's president should have

(B) being that the president of the organization should have

(C) was that the organization's president should have

(D) were that the organization's president has had

(E) was that the organization's president having

152

Improving Sentences

Choose the best way to revise the underlined part of the sentence. Your choice should make the most effective sentence and express the meaning of the original sentence. If no revision is needed, choose (A), which repeats the original underlined sentence part.

With a fresh blanket of snow on the ground and more to come, the principal had to determine <u>about closing the school</u> that day.

(A) about closing the school

(B) whether school is to be closed

(C) whether school was to be closed by her

(D) if closing school

(E) whether or not to close the school

153

Improving Sentences

> Choose the best way to revise the underlined part of the sentence. Your choice should make the most effective sentence and express the meaning of the original sentence. If no revision is needed, choose (A), which repeats the original underlined sentence part.

The first item for discussion on the agenda <u>which was whether the school implements</u> a dress code, or if a dress code would impose unnecessarily strict limitations.

(A) which was whether the school implements

(B) which being if the school should implement

(C) is to be should the school implement

(D) was whether the school should implement

(E) was if the school implemented

154

Improving Sentences

Choose the best way to revise the underlined part of the sentence. Your choice should make the most effective sentence and express the meaning of the original sentence. If no revision is needed, choose (A), which repeats the original underlined sentence part.

Anna's new watch is not waterproof, <u>which limitation makes it impractical for her</u>, since she is an avid swimmer.

(A) which limitation makes it impractical for her

(B) this being a practical limitation

(C) making it impractical for her

(D) that makes it impractical for her

(E) and as a result of this, being impractical for her

155

© 2006 Walch Publishing

Improving Sentences

Choose the best way to revise the underlined part of the sentence. Your choice should make the most effective sentence and express the meaning of the original sentence. If no revision is needed, choose (A), which repeats the original underlined sentence part.

Although the calendar says that it is the middle of spring, the unusual cold snap <u>makes it feel as though it is</u> the dead of winter.

        (A) makes it feel as though it is

        (B) is to make it feel like being

        (C) making it feel as though it is

        (D) makes it feel though it is

        (E) has made a feeling of its being

156

Improving Sentences

Choose the best way to revise the underlined part of the sentence. Your choice should make the most effective sentence and express the meaning of the original sentence. If no revision is needed, choose (A), which repeats the original underlined sentence part.

The first few days of Michael's new job <u>was a blur, as he struggled</u> to learn a new computer system and to familiarize himself with his coworkers.

(A) was a blur, as he struggled

(B) were a blur, as he struggled

(C) were a blur, struggles

(D) being a blur, as he struggled

(E) was a blur; as he struggled

157

Improving Sentences

Choose the best way to revise the underlined part of the sentence. Your choice should make the most effective sentence and express the meaning of the original sentence. If no revision is needed, choose (A), which repeats the original underlined sentence part.

<u>Being as she is an accomplished cellist,</u> Julia hopes to form a string quartet with a few other musicians.

      (A) Being as she is an accomplished cellist,

      (B) In being an accomplished cellist,

      (C) Although she is an accomplished cellist,

      (D) An accomplished cellist,

      (E) A cellist, also accomplished,

158

Improving Sentences

Choose the best way to revise the underlined part of the sentence. Your choice should make the most effective sentence and express the meaning of the original sentence. If no revision is needed, choose (A), which repeats the original underlined sentence part.

With this season's heavy rainfall, beach <u>erosion is an increasing concern</u>.

(A) erosion is an increasing concern

(B) erosion, increasing in concern

(C) erosion is, as a concern, increasingly

(D) erosion as a concern is increasing more

(E) erosion, an increasing concern

159

Improving Sentences

Choose the best way to revise the underlined part of the sentence. Your choice should make the most effective sentence and express the meaning of the original sentence. If no revision is needed, choose (A), which repeats the original underlined sentence part.

Hybrids made up of domestic and wild cats are growing in <u>popularity, many people are</u> concerned about their suitability as pets.

      (A) popularity, many people are

      (B) popularity; with many people

      (C) popularity, it is the case that many people are

      (D) popularity; concerning people

      (E) popularity, but many people are

160

Improving Paragraphs

Read the following unedited passage from an essay. It may need to be revised to improve organization, development, sentence structure, use of language, or use of standard English. Choose the answer that most improves the passage.

(1) <u>I have an unusual business, it has led me to meet</u> some very interesting people. (2) I make my living collecting family histories. (3) I conduct extensive interviews, and carefully preserve records of family lore.

Which of the following is the best way to phrase the underlined portion of sentence 1 (reproduced below)?

I have an unusual business, it has led me to meet some very interesting people.

(A) (As it is now)

(B) And so it's my unusual business that has led me to

(C) You see, then, I have an unusual business and as a result I meet

(D) Because I have an unusual business, I meet

(E) I should be meeting, naturally because I have an unusual business,

161

© 2006 Walch Publishing

Improving Paragraphs

Read the following unedited passage from an essay. It may need to be revised to improve organization, development, sentence structure, use of language, or use of standard English. Choose the answer that most improves the passage.

(1) When I first explain to people what I do, they are often quite surprised. (2) They find it difficult to believe that anybody would pay to have family stories recorded. (3) Likewise, few people seem to get around to doing it on their own, even though they plan to do so.

In context, which is the best way to deal with sentence 3 (reproduced below)?

Likewise, few people seem to get around to doing it on their own, even though they plan to do so.

(A) Change "seem" to "seems."

(B) Insert "But" at the beginning of the sentence.

(C) Change "Likewise" to "Still."

(D) Insert "by themselves" after "on their own."

(E) Change "plan" to "planning."

162

Improving Paragraphs

Read the following unedited passage from an essay. It may need to be revised to improve organization, development, sentence structure, use of language, or use of standard English. Choose the answer that most improves the passage.

(1) When I record a family history, I spend the most time with the elder members of a family. (2) Often, their own children and grandchildren are surprised to hear the stories they tell. (3) Believe that I help bring families closer together through my work.

In context, which of the following should be inserted at the beginning of sentence 3 (reproduced below)?

Believe that I help bring families closer together through my work.

(A) You should

(B) I like to

(C) Although,

(D) As such,

(E) For example,

163

Improving Paragraphs

Read the following unedited passage from an essay. It may need to be revised to improve organization, development, sentence structure, use of language, or use of standard English. Choose the answer that most improves the passage.

(1) As technology advances, people are increasingly able to work nontraditional schedules. (2) And they can work from locations other than the office.

Which of the following is the best way to revise and combine sentences (1) and (2)?

(A) (As it is now)

(B) As technology advances, people increasingly able to work nontraditional schedules are from locations other than the office.

(C) People being increasingly able to work nontraditional schedules, they can work from locations other than the office as technology advances.

(D) As with advancing technology, people are increasingly working nontraditional schedules, as well as, working from locations other than the office.

(E) As technology advances, people are increasingly able to work nontraditional schedules from locations other than the office.

164

Improving Paragraphs

Read the following unedited passage from an essay. It may need to be revised to improve organization, development, sentence structure, use of language, or use of standard English. Choose the answer that most improves the passage.

(1) Flexible schedules can be an excellent way for workers and employers to maximize their productivity. (2) Difficulties can arise if employers are not clear about their expectations.

In context, which of the following revisions is necessary in sentence 2?

(A) Insert ", however," after "arise."

(B) Insert "Because" at the beginning of the sentence.

(C) Change "can arise" to "were raised."

(D) Delete "their."

(E) Insert "and spell them out" after "expectations."

Improving Paragraphs

Read the following unedited passage from an essay. It may need to be revised to improve organization, development, sentence structure, use of language, or use of standard English. Choose the answer that most improves the passage.

(1) Employees need to know whether they are expected to keep regular business hours, even if they are working from home. (2) The clearer they are, the better able employees will be to meet expectations.

In context, which of the following most logically replaces "they" in sentence 2?

(A) these people

(B) work environments

(C) the rules

(D) these ideas

(E) some offices

166

Improving Paragraphs

Read the following unedited passage from an essay. It may need to be revised to improve organization, development, sentence structure, use of language, or use of standard English. Choose the answer that most improves the passage.

(1) Employees can do their part to help create a productive situation when they are working from remote locations.
(2) Communication, of course, being essential to any work relationship, and it is particularly so when the employee spends most of his or her time out of the office.

In context, which of the following revisions is necessary in sentence 2?

(A) Change "Communication" to "Communicate."

(B) Change "being" to "is."

(C) Delete "relationship."

(D) Change "his or her" to "they."

(E) Delete "of the office."

167

Improving Paragraphs

Read the following unedited passage from an essay. It may need to be revised to improve organization, development, sentence structure, use of language, or use of standard English. Choose the answer that most improves the passage.

(1) To foster a healthy work relationship, there are several points that employers should discuss with employees working from remote locations. (2) For example, how much time can elapse between communications? (3) How frequently should the employee update the employer? (4) Some people think that working outside the office is too much trouble. (5) Employers and employees should also agree on an appropriate method of performance evaluation.

What should be done with sentence 4 (reproduced below)?

Some people think that working outside the office is too much trouble.

(A) Leave it as it is.

(B) Delete it.

(C) Insert "As a result" at the beginning.

(D) Add "There is always the fact that" at the beginning.

(E) Add "and maybe they're right" at the end.

168

Improving Paragraphs

Read the following unedited passage from an essay. It may need to be revised to improve organization, development, sentence structure, use of language, or use of standard English. Choose the answer that most improves the passage.

(1) Granting employees flexible hours and remote locations can greatly benefit employers. (2) For example, when some or all of their staff members work from home, employers can pay for far less office space.

What should be done with sentence 2?

(A) Leave it as it is.

(B) Replace "For example" with "As a result."

(C) Insert "because of that" after "For example."

(D) Change "work" to "working."

(E) Rephrase the sentence and begin with "It is always the case that."

169

Improving Paragraphs

> Read the following unedited passage from an essay. It may need to be revised to improve organization, development, sentence structure, use of language, or use of standard English. Choose the answer that most improves the passage.

(1) Perhaps the greatest benefit of working remotely is the increased satisfaction that many employees report. (2) With less time spent commuting, they feel more focused on their jobs. (3) As well, they have more free time outside of work hours.

In context, which of the following is the best way to revise and combine sentences 2 and 3?

170

(A) Leave it as it is.

(B) When they spend less time commuting, they feel more focused on their jobs and plus they have more free time outside of work hours.

(C) Outside of work hours, with less time spent commuting, they feel more focused on their jobs.

(D) With less time spent commuting, they feel more focused on their jobs and also have more free time outside of work hours.

(E) They have more time with less commuting and feeling focused.

Improving Paragraphs

Read the following unedited passage from an essay. It may need to be revised to improve organization, development, sentence structure, use of language, or use of standard English. Choose the answer that most improves the passage.

(1) My family has been thinking about adopting a pet. (2) <u>Having some trouble agreeing</u> on the right type of animal for us.

In context, which of the following is the best version of the underlined portion of sentence 2?

(A) (As it is now)

(B) Some trouble has been had agreeing

(C) Agreeing, there has been trouble

(D) Having had some trouble we can't agree

(E) We have had some trouble agreeing

171

© 2006 Walch Publishing

Improving Paragraphs

Read the following unedited passage from an essay. It may need to be revised to improve organization, development, sentence structure, use of language, or use of standard English. Choose the answer that most improves the passage.

(1) My sister is trying to persuade my parents that we should get an exotic <u>bird. (2) It would perhaps be</u> a cockatiel or a macaw.

Which of the following is the best version of the underlined portion of sentences 1 and 2?

(A) (As it is now)

(B) bird, perhaps

(C) bird. Which would be perhaps

(D) bird, it would perhaps be

(E) bird, being perhaps

172

Improving Paragraphs

Read the following unedited passage from an essay. It may need to be revised to improve organization, development, sentence structure, use of language, or use of standard English. Choose the answer that most improves the passage.

(1) My father has his own ideas about the type of pet our family should get. (2) My sister, however, is allergic to them.

Which sentence is best to add after sentence 1?

(A) He believes that every family should have a dog.

(B) He has a lot of ideas, but he rarely follows through on them.

(C) My mother disagrees with him.

(D) Of course, he and my brother never feel the same way about anything.

(E) He mentioned a few different options that we can consider.

173

Improving Paragraphs

Read the following unedited passage from an essay. It may need to be revised to improve organization, development, sentence structure, use of language, or use of standard English. Choose the answer that most improves the passage.

My brother being unable to decide whether he would prefer to have a cat or a dog.

Which is the best way to revise this sentence?

    (A) Change "My brother" to "He."

    (B) Insert "he is" after "brother."

    (C) Change "being" to "is."

    (D) Delete "would."

    (E) Change "have" to "be having."

174

Improving Paragraphs

Read the following unedited passage from an essay. It may need to be revised to improve organization, development, sentence structure, use of language, or use of standard English. Choose the answer that most improves the passage.

(1) I tried to settle the dispute about what type of pet my <u>family should get. (2) I pointed out</u> that tropical fish are beautiful and less work than a dog or cat.

Which of the following is the best version of the underlined portion of sentences 1 and 2?

(A) family should get, and I pointed out

(B) family should get, and so pointed out

(C) family should be getting, because I pointed out

(D) family should get by pointing out

(E) family should then get, I pointed out

175

Improving Paragraphs

Read the following unedited passage from an essay. It may need to be revised to improve organization, development, sentence structure, use of language, or use of standard English. Choose the answer that most improves the passage.

(1) Whatever choice my family makes about a pet, one thing is certain. (2) <u>Getting any type of animal</u>, all of us will be responsible for its care.

In context, which is the best version of the underlined portion of sentence 2?

      (A) (As it is now)

      (B) In getting a type of animal

      (C) No matter what type of animal we get

      (D) Not that it matters what type of animal we get

      (E) If there is any type of animal gotten

176

Improving Paragraphs

Read the following unedited passage from an essay. It may need to be revised to improve organization, development, sentence structure, use of language, or use of standard English. Choose the answer that most improves the passage.

(1) A sheaf of letters that my great-grandfather wrote had been hidden away in a box in the attic for almost a hundred years. (2) Nobody had even known they existed. (3) Now, suddenly, we had a record of our ancestors' everyday lives.

Which of the following, if inserted before sentence 1, would make a good introduction to the paragraph?

(A) My family has a very interesting history.

(B) Some people make a hobby of researching their family history.

(C) My relatives came to America from several countries spanning Europe and Asia.

(D) Recently, I was thrilled to come across a family treasure.

(E) My family's future is uncertain, and its past even more so.

177

Improving Paragraphs

Read the following unedited passage from an essay. It may need to be revised to improve organization, development, sentence structure, use of language, or use of standard English. Choose the answer that most improves the passage.

(1) In reading my great-grandfather's letters, we discovered that he had some ideas that were ahead of his time. (2) It was that he wanted to invent a telephone that could transmit pictures. (3) This, of course, was long before televisions, computers, and fax machines existed.

In context, which of the following most logically replaces "It" in sentence 2?

(A) One such idea

(B) This idea

(C) The ideas

(D) This belief

(E) A thought he had

Improving Paragraphs

> Read the following unedited passage from an essay. It may need to be revised to improve organization, development, sentence structure, use of language, or use of standard English. Choose the answer that most improves the passage.

(1) We discovered, reading my great-grandfather's letters, that he'd had several get-rich-quick schemes. (2) Unfortunately, they had never seemed to work. (3) Still, he remained optimistic, always believing that he was just about to become very wealthy. (4) What seemed like a large sum of money back then would be very little now.

What should be done with sentence 4?

(A) Leave it as it is.

(B) Delete it.

(C) Insert "In spite of this," at the beginning of the sentence.

(D) Add "but he could not have known that" at the end.

(E) Rephrase the sentence and begin with "During that time."

179

Improving Paragraphs

Read the following unedited passage from an essay. It may need to be revised to improve organization, development, sentence structure, use of language, or use of standard English. Choose the answer that most improves the passage.

It was fascinating to learn so much about my family history, we learned this because of a stack of long-forgotten letters.

Which of the following is the best way to deal with this sentence?

(A) Change "fascinating" to "nice."

(B) Delete the comma after "history."

(C) Change "so much" to "this amount."

(D) Insert a comma after "this."

(E) Replace "we learned this" with "all."

Essay Prompts
1–30. Answers will vary.

Vocabulary-in-Context Practice

31.	C	36.	C
32.	D	37.	E
33.	B	38.	A
34.	D	39.	B
35.	E	40.	C

Sentence Completions

41.	B	50.	E
42.	A	51.	C
43.	D	52.	A
44.	E	53.	D
45.	C	54.	A
46.	C	55.	B
47.	B	56.	E
48.	D	57.	C
49.	A	58.	A

59.	E	65.	B
60.	D	66.	B
61.	C	67.	D
62.	D	68.	E
63.	E	69.	C
64.	A	70.	A

Passage-Based Reading

71.	D	83.	B
72.	B	84.	C
73.	A	85.	D
74.	E	86.	A
75.	B	87.	B
76.	C	88.	A
77.	C	89.	D
78.	A	90.	E
79.	D	91.	B
80.	E	92.	C
81.	E	93.	C
82.	C	94.	D

95.	C	98.	C
96.	E	99.	A
97.	D	100.	C

Identifying Sentence Errors

101.	C	116.	C
102.	C	117.	A
103.	B	118.	C
104.	A	119.	A
105.	D	120.	C
106.	D	121.	D
107.	C	122.	D
108.	E	123.	A
109.	E	124.	E
110.	E	125.	E
111.	A	126.	C
112.	D	127.	D
113.	A	128.	B
114.	E	129.	C
115.	B	130.	B

Improving Sentences

131.	E	146.	B
132.	D	147.	D
133.	C	148.	E
134.	B	149.	A
135.	E	150.	C
136.	C	151.	B
137.	B	152.	C
138.	A	153.	E
139.	C	154.	D
140.	A	155.	C
141.	D	156.	A
142.	A	157.	B
143.	B	158.	D
144.	C	159.	A
145.	E	160.	E

Improving Paragraphs

161.	D	164.	E
162.	C	165.	A
163.	B	166.	C

167.	B	174.	C
168.	B	175.	D
169.	A	176.	C
170.	D	177.	D
171.	E	178.	A
172.	B	179.	B
173.	A	180.	E

Turn downtime into learning time!

For information on other titles in the

Daily _Warm-Ups_ series,

visit our web site: walch.com